THE TEACHING OF READING

THE BURTON LECTURE

1956

The Teaching of Reading:
An International View

William S. Gray

Emeritus Professor of Education
The University of Chicago

HARVARD UNIVERSITY PRESS · CAMBRIDGE, MASS.
1957

LIBRARY OF CONGRESS CATALOG CARD NUMBER 58-6579
PRINTED IN THE UNITED STATES OF AMERICA

The Burton Lectureship

In order to stimulate interest and research in elementary education, Dr. and Mrs. William H. Burton gave to the Graduate School of Education, Harvard University, a fund for the maintenance of a lectureship under which a distinguished scholar or leader would be invited each year to discuss national problems in this field. A lectureship was accordingly established by the Graduate School of Education and named in honor of the donors. Dr. Burton, who was Director of Apprentice Teaching at Harvard for sixteen years, taught for forty-three years in the fields of elementary education and teacher education. It is hoped that these lectures will help to advance a study to which he is devoted and to which he has made distinguished contributions.

The Burton Lecturers

1955   Hollis L. Caswell. *How Firm a Foundation? An Appraisal of Threats to the Quality of Elementary Education.*

1956   William S. Gray. *The Teaching of Reading, an International View.*

1957   George Dearborn Spindler. *The Transmission of American Culture.*

THE TEACHING OF READING:
AN INTERNATIONAL VIEW

Current World-Wide Interest in Reading

AT no previous period in history has interest in reading been so universal or intense as it is today. Reports from abroad show that practically every nation, language, and culture is making vigorous efforts to help children and adults acquire either initial reading ability or greater competence in reading. This is due largely to two facts: a clear recognition among all nations of the tremendous role that world-wide literacy could play in promoting individual welfare, social progress, and international understanding; and the increasing demands made on readers in all literate countries for more discriminating choices and more penetrating interpretations of what is read. The varied reading problems which as a nation we face today are due, largely, to the same compelling forces.

Without doubt, the most spectacular developments in reading during recent years relate to world-wide efforts to eliminate illiteracy. The size of the task faced at the elementary school level is indicated by facts revealed through an international study of the extent of education among children of school age.[1] They show that out of every ten children in the world, only five go to school. Of these, four are in the primary grades and only one at the post-primary level. Other studies show that almost half of the adults of the world are wholly illiterate and not more than one-third have attained functional literacy, that is, the level of reading ability normally attained during at least four full years of schooling.[2] In view of the great contributions that reading might make to human welfare, this situation is appalling. Even in our own country, the portion of the adult population who have not attained functional literacy is 11.0 per cent, varying by states from 3.9 to 28.7 per cent.[3]

Recent Efforts to Extend Literacy

Although people have been taught to read for 4000 years or more, the effort to promote literacy on a world-wide scale is of relatively recent

[1] UNESCO, *World Survey of Education* (Paris, 1955), pp. 13–31.
[2] UNESCO, *Progress of Literacy in Various Countries* (Paris, 1953) Monographs in Fundamental Education, VI.
[3] William S. Gray, "How Well Do Adults Read?" *Adult Reading* (David H. Clift, Chairman), p. 38. Fifty-fifth Yearbook, National Society for the Study of Education, Part II (University of Chicago Press, 1956).

origin. The pioneers of the current movement [4] include such men as Jimmy Yen who began his work in France during World War I among Chinese illiterates who found themselves in a strange culture without means of communication; Frank Laubach, an American missionary, who began in the twenties to teach reading to the Moros in the Philippine Islands and has ever since carried on literacy campaigns among more than two-hundred different language groups which previously had no written language; Lorenco Filho, who for many years directed literacy drives among adult illiterates in Brazil; and Jaime Torres-Bodet, former Minister of Education in Mexico, who promoted a mass "each one teach one" movement among both children and adults in rural areas of that country.

The experiences of these and other inspired leaders led to two important conclusions. The first was that any training in reading that merely teaches the learner to recognize the forms and sounds of letters and to collate sounds in the pronunciation of words falls far short of the broader personal and social goals sought through reading. The second is that illiteracy is but one of many factors that contribute to the unfortunate conditions that now prevail in many coun-

[4] William W. Beatty, "Half the World Can't Read," *Phi Delta Kappan*, XXXVII (June 1956), 386–395.

tries and cultures and that serve as a menace to world peace.

When World War II came to an end the plight of millions upon millions of people stood out in tragic relief. Studies made in many areas showed that the inhabitants of these areas were not only illiterate but victims of poverty, superstition, malnutrition, endemic diseases, archaic methods of farming, lack of opportunity for self-government, and exploitation by nonresident landowners. Furthermore, they felt insecure, were greatly dissatisfied, and had adopted hostile attitudes. They had learned during the war that better conditions existed elsewhere. They were eager to improve their status but lacked the necessary knowledge and skills.

As efforts were made to improve such conditions, many plans developed which now bear such names as "social education" in India, "mass education" in Indonesia and China, "basic education" in Thailand, "community education" in the Philippines, and "fundamental education," directed by UNESCO in many parts of the world. The immediate purpose of these efforts has usually been to help people solve their most urgent problems; for example, to extend sanitation, reduce disease, produce more and better crops, improve the feeding and care of children.

At first, use was made of every concrete

means available to help individuals and groups understand and solve their problems. This plan was adopted in the belief that ideas are usually grasped more easily and clearly when presented in various ways, such as through demonstrations, posters, discussions, films, and the radio. Through skillful guidance, however, individuals and groups soon learned that the use of newspapers, pamphlets, and books is also of great value in any continued effort to solve their problems and to improve their status. As a result, "a burning desire" developed to be able to read and thus to have access to the many values and pleasures that may be secured through reading. The current world-wide drive to extend literacy has therefore become intimately related to efforts to help groups solve the immediate personal and community problems which they face. It differs notably from earlier campaigns which conceived literacy largely as an end in itself or as a badge of respectability.

New Needs and Issues Emerge

When literacy training began in most under-developed communities, attention was focused at first on the needs of the adults. In a short time, however, children began to attend literacy classes because they, too, were eager to learn to read and write. In efforts to teach mixed groups, it soon became evident that classes or schools adapted to the special needs of children were essential. The establishment of such schools marks a notable step forward, because the hope of a literate world tomorrow lies in the attainment of functional literacy on the part of the present generation of children.

As primary schools were established, the view was adopted that the curriculum followed should be community-centered. For example, the *1950 Yearbook* of the Philippine Association of School Superintendents states that, "the activities of the schools go far beyond the limits of the school compound and reach the homes, the occupations, the leisure activities of the people, and all the other aspects of social living. Its subject matter is not the books but the life which the children and the adults live. Its activities are those of living instead of imitating life." [5] It follows that the content used in teaching pupils to read also provides them with the knowledge and skills needed to live efficiently in their respective communities, and in today's world at large.

In efforts to achieve these challenging goals both in primary schools and in adult classes, it

[5] Philippine Association of School Superintendents, "Education in Rural Areas for Better Living," *1950 Yearbook* (Manila: Bookman, Inc., 1951), p. 5.

soon became evident that traditional procedures and standards in teaching reading were woefully inadequate. As a result, challenging questions arose concerning the nature of the reforms needed. None of these problems was more perplexing than the choice of appropriate methods in teaching beginners to read. This was due to the fact that the methods in use differed radically in their basic assumptions. Each had its ardent advocates and severe critics. As a result, confusion and uncertainty prevailed everywhere. The bitter controversy which has occurred recently in this country is but a reflection of the world-wide discussion since early in the forties concerning the relative merits of different methods of teaching children and adults to read.

Plans Adopted for a World-Wide Study

By 1949 so many urgent appeals for help in clarifying the situation had been filed with the United Nations that its General Assembly passed a resolution requesting UNESCO to provide needed information and directives.[6] Following several preliminary studies, the General Confer-

[6] William S. Gray, *Preliminary Survey of Methods of Teaching Reading and Writing*, Part I, p. 3. Educational Studies and Documents V, July 1953 (Paris, France: The Clearing House, UNESCO).

ence of UNESCO at its Sixth Session (1951)
authorized the Director General to make pro-
visions for a study of methods of teaching both
reading and handwriting which would continue
throughout 1952–1954. The tentative aims of the
first stage of this study with respect to reading
were defined thus:

1. To identify, analyze, and describe the various methods now used in teaching children and
adults to read.

2. To secure evidence concerning the effectiveness of these methods, wherever it is available.

3. To summarize the findings of the survey,
to consider their implications for the improve-
ment of reading, and to point out problems
meriting further research.

It was my good fortune to be asked to participate in this study.[7] While focusing attention on
the specific aims just described, I was at liberty
to identify practices and problems at all grade
levels and in countries at various stages of educational advancement. In securing needed information, I examined, through the assistance of
translators, the wealth of documentary material
from many countries that was on file in
UNESCO House in Paris, the University of

[7] William S. Gray, *The Teaching of Reading and Writ-
ing: An International Survey*, Monographs in Fundamental
Education X (Paris: UNESCO, 1956; Chicago: Scott,
Foresman).

London, and the Library of the International Bureau of Education in Geneva.

I also visited experimental centers in Geneva and Brussels, studied at firsthand the practices in teaching reading in several countries of Western Europe, and had either previously visited or now made field trips to Brazil, Cuba, Egypt, Puerto Rico, and Mexico. I also conferred with educational leaders from many countries and received questionnaire returns and reading materials from scores of field workers in countries with high literacy rates and in underdeveloped areas in all parts of the world.

Effect of the Diversity of Language on the Reading Act

As I studied the literature and instructional materials described above, I was overwhelmed both by their volume and the great number of languages represented. I was also greatly perplexed by the wide diversity in the form and structure of the written languages examined. A review of pertinent literature showed that there are about 2800 different languages in use today, exclusive of hundreds of minor dialects, and that they have been grouped in many different ways. Of special value with respect to the teaching of reading is their classification into three groups on the basis of the types of characters used in writing. In the order of their historical development, they are:

1. Word-concept characters, as in Chinese, each character representing a word, and some characters having several meanings according to the context in which they are used.

2. Syllabic-sound characters, as in Japanese, each character representing the sound of a syllable which may consist of a single phoneme or group of phonemes. These characters are used along with Chinese characters in writing Japanese.

3. Letter-sound characters, as in all alphabetic languages, each letter representing a phoneme or basic sound of a language. Depending on how well a language is spelled, the relationship between the letters used and the basic sounds of the respective languages is more or less invariable.

Further study revealed the fact that the methods used in teaching reading vary in many significant respects with the kinds of characters used in different languages. In teaching the reading of Chinese, for example, almost exclusive use was made formerly of so-called see-and-say methods of teaching. In the case of alphabetic languages, on the other hand, more or less emphasis has usually been given, sooner or later, to the sounds of letters as aids in word recognition.

Variations in methods of teaching arise from the fact that the number of letters used in written languages ranges from twelve to forty-five or more. Languages having relatively few letters are learned, as a rule, much more easily and quickly than those having many letters. In some languages each letter represents only one sound; in other languages, a given letter may represent one or more sounds. Furthermore, languages differ in the way in which the vowel sounds are represented, namely by separate letters as in English; by special marks which are attached to the consonants with which the vowels are collated, as in Arabic; and by internal modifications in the letter with which a vowel is associated.

The foregoing list of differences could be greatly expanded to include those relating to word order, inflection, and the manner of printing words—that is, separately as in "a boy hit the ball" or run together as in "aboyhittheball." Since many of these variations call for the use of special techniques or procedures in teaching, the question arises: Are there any common characteristics or principles on which the teaching of reading throughout the world can be based?

As I reflected on this problem I recalled that early investigators who secured photographic records of eye-movements in reading had found that the basic steps or processes involved were similar in the case of mature readers of English, French, and German. These findings suggested that if this were true also of mature readers of other languages, common guides in the teaching of reading might be identified. I was discouraged at first from undertaking such a study by consultants from many countries, who believed that the habits and skills involved in reading different languages vary with their form and structure. Some of them also maintained that the reading of their own language, even at the mature level, was a synthetic process which consisted of collating the sounds of letters in proper order rather than a process of grasping words as wholes.

Nevertheless, I spent several months in securing eye-movement records of mature readers from fourteen different countries, using the same passages translated into the following languages: Arabic, Burmese, Chinese, English, French, Hebrew, Hindi, Japanese, Korean, Navaho, Spanish, Thai, Urdu, and Yoruba (a Nigerian language). In making selections I tried to include as wide a representation as possible of written languages differing in both form and structure.

The eye-movement records that were secured [8] supplied striking evidence that the basic processes involved in reading are similar the

[8] Gray, *The Teaching of Reading and Writing: An International Survey*, pp. 55–60.

world over, independent of the language read, its structure, or the kinds of characters or letters used. They also refuted the idea that the perception of words by good readers in any language is basically a process of identifying and collating the sounds of their various parts. Instead, most words are perceived instantly as wholes, often in units of two or three, as the eyes progress along the lines in a series of successive movements and pauses. When, however, a new or difficult word is met, the good reader makes more-or-less use of analysis in recognizing it. Further study of the records showed that word perception in all languages involves at least three basic aspects: the accurate recognition of the meaning and pronunciation of symbols; a wide span of recognition; and the instantaneous perception of words and groups of words. In addition, it was found that good readers everywhere read silently more rapidly than orally, and that the processes involved in the two types of reading differ in similar respects.

Purposes of Reading and Essential Interpretive Processes

These finding were very illuminating and suggested many common objectives and guides in developing word-perception skills. But the recognition of words is only one important aspect of reading. Before attempting to evaluate current methods of teaching, it seemed desirable to know more about the purposes that stimulate people to read and the reading attitudes and skills needed. Accordingly, a summary was made of hundreds of statements of purposes for reading reported from different areas of the world.

A group of natives in South Africa, for example, stated that they read to keep in touch with their families; to locate streets and buildings; to observe danger signals on the street and at work; to follow simple directions; to obtain needed information; to keep up with current happenings; and to read little books on "how-to-do-it," healthy living, best foods to eat, and better ways of farming. Reports from Thailand indicated that in addition to the purposes just mentioned, people read to learn more about their businesses or vocations and to attain greater economic independence; to keep in touch with developments in their country and to learn more about its ideals and aspirations; to understand social, political, and economic changes, and to participate in the solution of related problems; and in the case of many young men, to prepare for the priesthood. In reports from India, special emphasis was given to the fact that all people must learn to read thoughtfully and critically if they are to be good citizens and to participate intelligently in developing a democracy adapted to their culture.

As the study continued, it became increasingly clear that motives for reading are similar in many respects the world over, differing primarily in extent of use rather than in kind. When an analysis was made of the attitudes and skills needed to attain the goals sought, it was found that they include the following among others: a thoughtful reading attitude; accurate and thorough comprehension; thoughtful reaction to what is read with appropriate emotional responses; and the integration of the ideas acquired with the reader's previous experiences. The last step mentioned is the heart of the learning act in reading and is essential if new and clearer understandings, rational attitudes, and improved thought and behavior patterns are to be acquired.

These findings challenge the validity of reading programs, in both underdeveloped and highly literate countries, that aim chiefly to promote word-recognition skills. Of major importance is the need also for clear understanding of what is read, including literal, related, and implied meanings; critical appraisal of the ideas acquired, including appropriate emotional apprehension; and the integration of what is read into the reader's store of information, attitudes, ideals, and motives. This point of view is further expanded by the following statement from India: "The reader must not only master the mechanics of reading but he must grow in his awareness of the social context of what he reads and of the forces operating in his environment. Only by these means can he understand and evaluate what he reads, make wise decisions and sense the direction of desirable social changes and governmental policies." [9]

Methods of Teaching Beginning Reading

With the foregoing concept of reading and its basic processes in mind, a survey was made of the methods used in teaching beginning reading. Relevant literature from various countries was reviewed, reports from field workers were studied, and more than two-hundred sets of materials used in teaching adults to read and the first books in a corresponding number of sets of readers for children were analyzed. In addition, observations were made of the teaching procedures used in both primary schools and literacy classes.

After consideration of various possible plans

[9] National Seminar on the Organization and Techniques for the Liquidation of Illiteracy, Jabalpur, 1950, *Report* (Delhi: Indian Adult Education Association, 1951), p. 46.

of classifying the hundreds of different methods identified, it seemed advisable to classify them on a historical basis. Accordingly, the first group consisted of highly specialized methods which had their origins in the remote or more recent past. These methods were of two general types. The first concentrates more-or-less exclusively from the beginning on the mastery of word elements which are then combined to form words in the reader's oral vocabulary and used in the recognition of unfamiliar words in reading lessons. This group includes the alphabetic, phonic, and syllabic methods. A second group makes use from the beginning of meaningful language units, such as words, sentences, stories, and group experiences, and cultivates persistently a thoughtful reading attitude. As soon as a basic sight vocabulary has been acquired, attention is directed to the elements of words, which in turn are used in recognizing new words. The latter step is introduced sooner or later and carried on with varying degrees of thoroughness.

The conflict between these two aproaches to reading is a classic one and has waged for centuries. During recent years two distinct trends have developed which have radically modified the methods of teaching used in many areas of the world. The first is the eclectic trend which emphasizes from the beginning both meaning and the skills of word recognition. In addition, an effort is made to emphasize all other aspects of reading essential in developing a good reader at the first-grade level. As a result teachers follow a broad reading program rather than a single method of teaching. This insures an adequate foundation on which later efforts to promote growth in reading can be based. The second trend is learner-centered in that the content selected for use relates directly to the child's interests and activities, and the methods used are adapted to the varying abilities and modes of learning of different pupils. These two trends are, in a sense, a product of the tested experience of the race.

The Relative Merits of Different Methods

Although the trends just described have been adopted with surprising rapidity during recent years, widely diverse views still prevail concerning the relative merits of different methods of teaching beginning reading. In an effort to resolve this conflict, the results of more than fifty pertinent experiments carried on in several countries were reviewed critically. In brief, they led to the following conclusions.[10]

[10] Gray, *The Teaching of Reading and Writing: An International Survey*, chap. vi.

1. Children have learned to read by almost any method that ingenious men and women have devised.

2. The available evidence does not show which specialized method is best, because all such methods have not been tried out experimentally and many of the studies reported have not been adequately controlled.

3. All children and adults do not learn to read equally well by a given method. This implies that there are factors other than the method used that influence progress in learning to read, such as the teacher, the home and school environment, and the varying abilities and other characteristics of learners.

4. Contrasting methods emphasize different aspects of reading and start children on different roads to maturity in reading. If word recognition receives exclusive emphasis, one set of attitudes and skills is developed; if meaning only is stressed, a different set is cultivated. Ultimately a reader must acquire all the attitudes and skills involved in efficient reading.

5. Progress in learning to read is most rapid when both meaning and the skills of word recognition are stressed from the beginning. The additional statement may be made that a sound reading program promotes growth in all the interests, understandings, attitudes, and skills that

characterize an efficient reader at each level of school progress.

The results of other types of studies reinforce the foregoing findings and supplement them to advantage. For example, it has been found that most children usually perceive things (including words) as wholes, often inaccurately at first, but gradually in greater detail. Furthermore, both children and adults learn words more quickly in context than in isolation and apply themselves to learning most effectively when the reading activities are purposeful and meaningful to them.

Such findings tend to limit the scope of the remaining controversial issues with respect to initial methods of teaching reading. With but very few exceptions, even the ardent advocates of the use of phonics are now basing the initial identification of letters and sounds on the study of word wholes. In Belgium, for example, all the phonetic elements of the language taught are learned through the study of about fifteen words of high interest value to pupils. As rapidly as a few of them are mastered, children apply them in writing other words in their oral vocabularies and in recognizing new words in reading. Likewise, teachers who employ the sentence or so-called "global method" of teaching reading are directing attention early to the details of words in reading lessons by writing them, typing them, or reproducing them through the use of small printing sets.

Of large importance is the fact that linguists, both in this country and abroad, recommend that initial training in reading should begin with word wholes. They insist, however, that various patterns of words should be learned before any reading is done. Furthermore, the letters of the words in each pattern should always have the same sounds (such as *bat*, *fat*, *hat*, *rat* and *fate*, *hate*, *mate*, *rate*). As soon as a series of such patterns have been taught, the child is given material to read which is restricted to the patterns that have been taught but not to the specific words learned. In the meantime, words that are spelled irregularly are introduced and learned separately. Thus, the area of controversy is moving from the merits of the highly specialized, traditional methods of teaching beginning reading to proposals of more recent origin. I anticipate that notable progress will be made during the next few years in experimental evaluations of the latter.

Reading Programs at More Advanced Levels

As we direct attention to the nature of reading programs above the primary level, we face the amazing fact that they are in their infancy in most areas of the world. On the basis of the data cited earlier, not more than 5 per cent of the children the world over and a surprisingly small percent of adults are receiving or have received training in reading above the primary-grade level. Among the countries that do provide more advanced training, the practices in teaching reading differ widely. As a basis for comparison, it may be helpful to review briefly the prevailing policies in this country.

One of the distinctive marks of progress during the last three decades has been the extension of systematic guidance in reading into high schools and colleges. The adoption of this plan was based on three established facts: first, that growth in reading is a continuous process from infancy to old age; second, that each successive period of development brings challenging demands that require new and higher levels of competence in reading; and third, that progress in acquiring needed competencies and in mastering the more mature aspects of reading is greatly facilitated through appropriate guidance. Accordingly, special effort is made at each stage of development to provide needed training in reading classes, in various curriculum fields, in the library, and if necessary, in remedial classes and clinics. As aids in achieving the goals sought, a wealth of professional literature, teachers' guides, and reports of pertinent research have been published.

A survey of all the available literature relating to reading abroad revealed only a limited number of discussions of reading problems above the primary grades. However, several countries of Western Europe and those in the British Commonwealth are now engaged in studies of the problems faced in the middle and upper grades and, to a limited extent, in high schools. Of larger importance is the fact that most English-speaking countries are making wide use of the literature and research findings of this country. In such cases, the methods used do not differ radically from our own, except in the extent of their application. In many of the other countries systematic training in reading is discontinued at the end of the first, second, or third school year. In other countries it is correlated with the teaching of the mother tongue or other school subjects.

As implied by the foregoing statements, much of the guidance in reading given above the earliest grades depends very largely on the training, experience, and insight of teachers. This is true in France, to use but a single example, which provides little supervision and few specific guidebooks for teachers. As pointed out by Jean Simon, "Whereas we [in France] rely on teacher interpretation, personal methods and intuition, the United States identifies specific stages and techniques including an elaborate system of guidance." [11] The fact that our own practices have been studied critically during recent years by representatives of many countries justifies the expectation that reading programs will be extended steadily upwards during the next decade in most areas of the world.

One might assume that because basal instruction in reading is discontinued early in many countries, there is little or no reading retardation abroad. Such is far from true. The most persistent question included in the reports from field workers everywhere was, what can be done to help the child or adult who has difficulty in learning to read? Furthermore, intensive studies have been published recently and others are now being made in most countries of Western Europe and in Japan to learn more concerning the causes and remedies of serious difficulties in learning to read.

Availability of Reading Materials

If the broader goals sought through reading are to be achieved, several requirements must be met far more adequately than at present in many

---

[11] Jean Simon, "The Teaching of Reading and Writing: An International Survey," *Elementary School Journal*, LVII (November 1956), 83–94.

countries. The first is a notable enrichment of reading materials. Experience in this country supplies striking evidence of the value of an abundance and varied types of reading material in promoting desirable reading interests and skills among both children and adults. As a result, a veritable flood of readers, workbooks, practice exercises, guidebooks, textbooks, supplementary materials, and library books have been published, particularly for children and youth. Very few, if any, other countries have made such generous provision. Teachers from abroad who visit our schools are very envious of both the quality and attractiveness of the reading materials found in most classrooms.

In striking contrast, many areas of the world have great difficulty in securing even a small paper- or cloth-bound primer, and possibly two or three more advanced readers, for use in teaching either children or adults to read. This is due in part to scarcity of paper. Equally important is the lack of qualified personnel to prepare basal reading materials. Until these limitations can be overcome, progress in developing functional literacy will be very slow.

Many of the more advanced countries are making notable progress, particularly in the preparation of basal readers. This was brought dramatically to my attention through studies made in the library of the International Bureau of Education, in Geneva, Switzerland. The librarian had arranged in chronological order readers from each of sixty or more countries that have been published over a period of three decades or more. As one examines this exhibit he is thrilled by the numerous evidences of progress since 1940: the increasing length of many series; the use of content that has vital meaning and significance to children; far more attractive covers and better art work within readers; and more careful selection and gradation of vocabulary. Similar changes, particularly in respect to learner-centered content, are occurring in basal reading materials for adults. These trends offer great promise for the future.

The importance of recreational or library reading materials is far less clearly recognized. A notable exception at the adult level is the work of the literature committees in Africa, which for many years have made a great contribution by providing reading materials based on the known interests of the adults served. Similar efforts are being made in portions of Spanish-speaking America. In most underdeveloped areas, however, very few reading materials are available for those who have completed their literacy training. Unfortunately, the Communists, particularly in parts of Asia, are taking advantage of this situation by providing simple bulletins in the various languages which aim to secure converts to their philosophy and form of government.

Considerable progress has been made in most countries of Western Europe in providing recreational books for children. As yet they lag far behind this country in the number, variety, and attractiveness of the books provided. In less well-developed parts of the world the needs of adults take precedence over those of children. The situation prevailing in the Arabic world is typical. While working on a project for the Ministry of Education in Egypt in 1950, I secured the coöperation of the librarians in Cairo in identifying the books in the Arabic language that were based on the interests of children and adolescents. Even when the content of books was very liberally interpreted fewer than two hundred titles were identified. Until this situation can be corrected, three-fourths of the children and youth of the world will not be able to use reading to any extent in enriching their experience, in securing wholesome pleasure, and in finding solutions to many personal or social problems.

The Urgent Need for Teachers

A second, almost-insuperable barrier to rapid progress in developing a literate world is the lack of teachers, either trained or untrained. Reports received from practically all underdeveloped areas stated again and again that lack of teachers and appropriate reading materials were the most serious handicaps faced. Native people will exert themselves to the maximum to provide buildings or compounds in which instruction can be given, but they have to rely for instruction on missionaries, social workers, and the few native literate people who are available. In India it has been estimated that two million additional elementary-school teachers and about five hundred thousand secondary-school teachers are needed immediately. When we contemplate the difficulties which we are having in this country in supplying our mounting needs for teachers, it is evident that the world faces a colossal task in achieving universal literacy.

Concluding Statement

As implied by the foregoing discussion, the world is passing through an epochal period today in respect to reading. Radical social and political changes during recent years have made rapid progess toward literacy a matter of great urgency. A "burning desire" to learn to read has swept over the world like a tidal wave. A broad concept of the nature of reading and of its basic steps and processes has emerged which has universal application. Detailed procedures in teaching reading must be developed in harmony with unique aspects of each language and the needs of each culture. The world today lacks personnel and facilities needed to teach the millions of children and adults who are as yet illiterate. The time required to attain world literacy depends on the rapidity and effectiveness with which these needs can be met.

I am often asked if there is anything that can be learned to our advantage from an international study of reading. In reply, I refer to three impressions that have been written indelibly on my mind. The first is the profound respect for reading as a vital aid to human welfare that prevails the world over. The second is the passionate desire to learn to read on the part of millions of children in underdeveloped areas, and in many literate countries as well, which results in a vigorous and sustained application in learning activities that we often fail to approximate. It is engendered in the home and further cultivated by various elements of the culture. The third is the great devotion of thousands of teachers abroad to the task of helping children learn to read and the high ideal of excellence which they inculcate and help pupils achieve. From these attributes of the mind, the heart, and the spirit, we can learn much.